Primo Vino

Other books by Rose Basile Green:

To Reason Why (Sonnets)
The Cabrinian Philosophy of Education
The Italian-American Novel
    A Document of the Interaction of Two Cultures

Primo Vino

Rose Basile Green

*To Sister Amedea, M.S.C.,
in memory of the hard
ploughing we shared in
the vineyard.
Affectionately,
Rose Basile Green*

April 15, 1975

South Brunswick and New York: A. S. Barnes and Company
London: Thomas Yoseloff Ltd

© 1974 by A. S. Barnes and Co., Inc.

A. S. Barnes and Co., Inc.
Cranbury, New Jersey 08512

Thomas Yoseloff Ltd
108 New Bond Street
London W1Y OQX, England

Library of Congress Cataloging in Publication Data

Green, Rose Basile, 1914–
Primo vino.

Poems.
1. Italians in the United States—Poetry. I. Title.
PS3557.R3754P7   811'.5'4   74-13593
ISBN 0-498-01660-9

PRINTED IN THE UNITED STATES OF AMERICA

Dedication

To the Ancestors: **Siamo Arrivati!**

Let us unplug our nonno's caraffone
That lay sack-wrapped below the cellar door,
And wash the grime until the film is gone
To show the crystal as it was before.
Fill up his hand-blown bottle to the brim
And pour the scarlet bubbles in each glass;
Give, with respect, a toast remembering him
In the fermented wine he brought to pass.
Touch goblets to recurring pioneers
Who always showed the world the newest beam;
And, having sweat their fears, dissolved their tears
To harvest in the sun their native dream.

Drink to their classic way we here revived;
Once more, in Saturn's ring, we have arrived.

Contents

Hall Of Fame

Conclusions

Preface

Prior to the nineteen sixties, the hyphenated American had nearly phased out as the result of years of assiduous and quiet effort to implement the machinery of assimilation. Today, however, engendered by the thrust of politico-social fragmentation, he finds himself restructured as an ethnic.

Ethnicity is pervasively one of the catchwords of contemporary society. With the healthy, persistent push of the black population for analysis, identity, and recognition, and with the increasing reality of the practical application of civil rights, all groups who feel circumscribed by a common tie are asserting themselves to be noticed and respected as part of the American concept as well as of the nation's statistical population. A definitive unity is seeking its amalgam through the absorption of diversity.

Italian-Americans are a large ethnic group. During the hundred years between 1822 and 1922, the immigrants from Italy were second in number only to those who came from Germany—close to five millions. Now, with the second, third, and fourth generations, Americans of Italian ancestry number somewhere between twenty and twenty-five millions. It is difficult to make the count. Some admit only to being American; others have acquired Anglo-Saxon names through marriage or simple adoption.

These Italian-Americans, wholly or in part, demonstrate endemic concepts that are emerging along with their social establishment. However, as an ethnic group they have a universal complaint. On May 10, 1971, in an essay entitled "The Age of Touchiness" in *Time* magazine, Melvin Maddocks wrote a parody of a protest letter to the *New York Times*. The substance of the letter registers a complaint that films, plays, and novels have portrayed a particular ethnic minority as a vicious stereotype that has nothing to do with the facts. Admitting the validity of this complaint, the Italian-American's real rancor is roused because of the distortion of his image.

In an attempt to convey the complexities that frame this need for a proper image—or, as they have said eternally in Rome—"la bella figura," I offer these verses to communicate the Italian-American's point of view. Some of these poems emphasize how Italian-Americans feel emotionally as an isolated, clustered group. Other poems are sympathetic observations of recalled persons, situations, and events of the American experience. Nothing is intended to be offensive, and nothing is intended to be defensive. There is cause for celebration.

RBG

Primo Vino

Primo Vino

Italians here are like the flow of wine,
The **Primo Vino** that ferments the grape;
Like pristine truths the oracles define,
They tap the source that gives the vision shape.
From grapes they press three grades of wine are drawn:
The first, the elixir of virgin birth;
The second, juiced until the skins are gone;
The third, a watery sludge of little worth.
In company, they celebrate the best,
For each the other values by his cup;
At home, the lesser is enough to rest;
While for the crowd the dredge is measured up.

They brought the cup to toast the new land's vine;
They broke the maidenhead, made first the wine.

To America

We sing America, this land we own;
The roots of nations in our language lies,
That our forebears in history made known
To give communication vocal ties.
As once the lands our fathers organized
To march the men from trees and caves to towers,
Then built the spires of ritual stone, devised
To lift man's eyes above his earthly bowers,
And then they led the minds to know again
The sources whence their flood of art had sprung,
So here they led their sails with borrowed pain
From which their claim refuses to be wrung.

America, we sing, this land is ours to bring
Once more the destined law from which all freedoms spring.

They Came Because

To get away was not their urgent cause,
For their Acadia was the garden spot
Where beauty caught wild butterflies, whose flaws
Seduced the laws to rule what they had not.
The wheat was burned; the vineyards all had dried;
The temples stripped of curves and Gothic arcs,
Beneath whose crumbled crowns the mothers cried
Where Emperors' tongues were silenced by the larks.
The cities, old, veil Alps and Apennines;
They footnote time with dusty pedigrees;
And, scaling tops of mountains in the pines,
Old crosses rule the landscape from the trees.

They came to do, with strength renew the cup they wrought;
With them the secret of the bread and wine they brought.

Parting

To say farewell to fatherland is death
To birth, the infancy, the milk of life.
The gentian-scented air that fans the breath
Is slaked within the vacuum of strife.
The dark-crowned youths leap on the parting trains
To spare themselves the final drowning gaze
That curtains land where woman's arm detains
And halts the westward veering of their days.
They leave the father's house, the mother's sighs,
The priestly chidings honing souls with wine,
Young wives with tears to feed their babies' cries;
For lack of bread, they thirst for ship and brine.

They loop the circle round, the braided human rope,
To lend once more their genius, freedom of their hope.

The Voyage

In steerage heaps they sailed to roosted shores,
Where buzzards fought with eagles from the rocks,
Upon whose crests the feathers sealed the doors
Of steel-veined towers seen from shrouded docks.
The voyage was at best a broken dream
Of fetid stench, with bodies bending tight
In sickness shared with swill and equine stream
Below the darkness of subhuman night.
The single light was in their gentle eyes
That bore the Senate stoics' fortitude;
The cross and tool sustained their stifled cries
To hope once more to decorate the rude.

Just as the sages must their infant rebels hold and feed,
So bent they low to every blow to fortify their seed.

Little Italy

There is a place called Little Italy,
A little to the east and to the south,
The channeled substream of geography,
That filters at the northern river's mouth.
The bocce courts, the pastry shops, the stalls,
All interlaced with statuettes and vines,
Are lesser models of old forum walls
And centered atria templed with old pines.
The houses, browned with stones of Nordic race,
Give little cue that, once within the door,
You step into the Renaissance and grace;
The world can give you little that is more.

The tabled circle sloughs the tankards of the west;
They drink their father's wine and find it still the best.

The Family

The family is a jury and a court,
The prosecutor and defender, each
A limbing from the judge that is a sort
Of tyrant, loving whom he must impeach.
Before the patriarch they hush and bow
As he a fury wields to bend each one;
And, yet, behind that dark and scowling brow
Are lights that warm them like the autumn sun.
The brothers check the sisters' levity
And guard the mother's holy-ghosted home,
The spirit of the table's trinity
To help as one the father's kingdom come.

Protecting unity, the generations wait,
Respecting loyalty, their shrine and syndicate.

The Father

Centurion! A tense internal roar—
He keeps alive in him his boyhood dream,
That he above the afternoon would soar
And rule the shifting West that banks the stream.
He drives the pilings with his work and pride
That in his art he is the best, no boor
At potions, courts, or pulpits, desks that ride
The dignity of man to make him poor.
Dantesque in scope, Byronic in his flair,
He rules the family court and public dins;
His mother's diadem now crowns his daughter's hair;
His Beatrice rewards the son who wins.

The dago, twisted from the doge's sinking realm,
Is still the discipline at both the stern and helm.

The Mother

She is the low-keyed chord beneath the blast,
The counterpoint that blends the harmony;
While to the theme her loyalty is fast,
Arpeggios stretch her staff's embroidery.
She decorates her virgin, feeds her son
With practice hours of ambition's tune;
And better than her piano there is none
To make their measured home so opportune.
The social cult that Henry Adams blest
The mathematics of our music scored;
In rhythm's melody she dressed
The off-pitched pedal of our alien board.

As, fogged at north, the crows are silenced by a thrush,
Her voice can mollify the clamor with its hush.

The Son

Staff Sargeant, grinding hard for captain's bars,
He made his leap by reining his own horse.
He shined his stirrups with the light of stars,
And trimmed the fetlocks strengthened by his force.
The midnight oil expands his borrowed light
From poetry, to history, to facts;
For some protection he may stoop in fright,
But stands before the colors and the pacts.
Now in the clubs he wears his wings and sheath
From every kind of race that he has run;
Beside him, pilot's wife with smoky wreath
Bestows the graces from the bowl he won.

The son of Eli or of some other don today,
With gentle hand picks up his case and rides his way.

24

The Daughter

The daughter is the agony of home,
The budding bearer of a plant unknown;
She must her calyx out of sight entomb
Although the petals urge a rose full blown.
Along the paths of town she must waft straight,
From living room to classroom in a line.
From school and church and parents deviate
No books, no beads, no measure of the vine.
As in her buried conscience Trojan women cry,
She weaves the gentle cloth for Pilate's hands.
The martyrs of her culture blend the dye
To etch the patterns of the shifting sands.

Although she plays an extra on the stage of family life,
She must at any moment know the role of Caesar's wife.

The Godfather

The Godfather is covenant of strength,
The tree on which young reason is a bud,
Whose branch can settle crime from one pure length
Instead of tricking for a nation's blood.
He is the ancient enterprise, ignored,
The subtle mind in field, at court, at home,
Whose wisdom in the afternoon he stored,
Unheeded by the prodigals of Rome.
And when new brigands shut to him their doors
That they may sanctify their rape and hoard,
They show contempt for history by wars
Of dog-flea quakes where older eagles soared.

The leader is the genius who can a nation hold
By hitting with a contract the cache the traitors sold.

Women's Names

Just listen to the sounds; they scale a song
From royal choirs to the music sheet.
Flavia, Claudia to the court belong;
The patron Catherine is a saint, a street.
Mafalda, Margherita royal were:
Imelde, Juno, Gloria and Ione;
But Beatrice the poet's dreams could stir,
While Juliet and pure Laura loved their own.
The Theresas, Veras, and Carmellas are
The nurses of Calpurnia's classic bower;
The queenly name is Gina, western star.
And Annes go Caroling with Linda's flower.

As Maria by Antonia is enhanced from mystic myrrh,
So Caroline is carried, magnified by Saxon burr.

Love and Wine

We live with love and pasta, bread and wine,
With texture firm, al dento, underdone;
For though the lavish hand bids you to dine,
The quantity by sapient taste is run.
And when you pour, fill not too much the glass
That you may not be able then to drink;
For, as the sips the brutish gulps surpass,
The half-filled glass leaves time to edge the brink.
Just as suggestion is the soul of verse,
The fraction that excites the metaphor,
So love is cupped in winy language, terse,
The whispered breath that scents the lover's door.

Italians have the stoic's careful, metered taste;
Their discipline—no love, no bread will fritter into waste.

Religion

The saints are older relatives and friends
Who carry keys to turn divinities;
Each Philomena everyone defends
Against the canon's regularities.
The eyes of men are narrowed at the priest,
Allowing gentle human frailties;
But of their homely hoard they give the least

And seldom whisper sins on bended knees.
As long ago in Rome the household gods
Were sharers in the rudest banquet brine,
So, still, the matrix to her sons rewards
Unleavened bread, the ferment of the wine.

There is no food they would not spare that others eat
There is no wine denied to make the memory sweet.

Superstition

Magic in the hands of brutes degenerates
To sorcery. In mumbo-jumbo, cant, and spells,
A chain of want and fear it operates
To blot the sky with clouds of poison cells.
As twisted minds brew nightmares out of dreams
Of times when fathers' gods the forum walked,
The people now chafe at the gothic seams
To hear the music the old Senate talked.
The evil eye reflects the underground
To which excruciation spirit kills;
The notes, that once were massed with Latin sound,
Reverberate the bongo drums of hills.

The elixir of art may be too fine, too rare,
For growth whose stunted buds demand the desert air.

Festa (San Gennaro)

You go to Catholic school, but do not know
Gennaro, brought to Inwood's afternoon,
Stretched late in strings of light, the afterflow,
The saddened features etched on a balloon.
The pushcarts, pennants, pizza stands, all treat
With capozzelli, ice, and zeppolone
The crowds from Mulberry to Bleeker Street,
Where plaster saints are wrapped with the calzone.
Improper fireworks without a piazza
Show not the noble faces, coats of arms
That once the Renaissance had fused the razza,
But now the noise of memory barely warms.

The mandolins, the feasts, the holy and sweet
      singing that you hear
Are antidotes to heal the loneliness, frustration,
      and the fear.

Italian-American Priesthood

You hide your light in tabernacles low,
While foggy gleams exaggerate the streams
Of spinning metaphysics that they know
Will serve the politics of drunken dreams.
Within the cellar doors you served the Mass
To black-garbed women in whose knowing eyes
The shades of wisdom still all things surpass
As did Minerva in her god-seat rise.
When late in Primavera Venus sprang
To add the human touch to abstract love,
The Church, the mind of Rome, New England sang
For other Botticellis man to move.

Among the bogs where exploitation used the bell,
You bore the cross that history made you build and sell.

The Newspapers

Progresso, Popolo, Corriere, all
The weeklies, monthlies, dailies, night and noon,
Their story stamped; the periodical
Which kept their guard against the known lampoon.
The pages inked the theses and the briefs,
The details of their banquets and their fares;
Between the lines, the annals of their griefs
Were sublimated in the print of wares.
DiMaggio's bat; LaGuardia in the field;
A judge is here, and there a politico;
The stories harvest large a scattered yield
To bolster up the vowel end of ego.

Theirs is the artifact the conflict wrought
In tensions of two systems cast and fought.

Grocery Stores

Venetian cloves waft near the saffron gold
And Lombard packs of bleached-out China rice;
Oregano stirs; whispers garlic hold
For phallic provoloni's urging spice.
Mild mozzarella, prosciutto, capo red
Enrich the wheat in macaroni shapes,
Or fill the crusts of oven-scented bread
That plump salsicci, peperoni, takes.
The blossomed greens, the flowered cippolines,
Mix pungent scents of aromatic herbs;
The peppers and tomatoes, plump lupines,
All overflow to sidewalks, mounding curbs.

Herein the savors of all time and lands enfold
The story that the tongue of man has prized and told.

Across the Tracks

Across the tracks they sought the ancient dream
That once was theirs and then eluded us;
And when they pioneered the bay and stream,
They soon removed the offal without fuss.
The scale in Grant Street has an empty sound
And mulberries have long since left the trees,
Where once the organ-grinder played the round
From street to street composing memories.
No passing train now whistles with the wind,
For silent was their exodus, and slow,
As each a mansion for his home would find,
Where quietly his children's children grow.

To lift the bread with wine from sterling cups with ease,
They offer neither shame nor late apologies.

The Old Neighborhood

The tentacles of memory clutch back
Like swamp-moss, hanging leaves the live-oaks bear;
They swing against the wind across the track
And catch the whiffs and sounds that once were there.
The chrome is thin veneer the Pizza Parlor flaunts
Where card games were preludes to syndicates;
The mobile toys of play yards hide old haunts
Where feasts of saints brought home the profligates.
The Zia's "Way," the old gumpa's "Walyo!"
Cut through the layered tones of graduate school;
Above the fire steps the fat cats go
Where once small boys stretched out their dreams to cool.

The old street bids like Nonna's bosom, fat and warm,
And offers its protective blanket with its arm.

Pastry Shops

Let us give praises to embellished bread
By beauty lifted from the sod and cane;
Gross hunger by plain wheat is eased and fed
But barely can the artist's taste sustain.
The flower exudes its perfume from the bower
And makes a garden where the grasses grow;
The magic of creative hands turns flour
Into the pasticieri that we know.
Sfigliatelli, canelloni, rum-soaked cakes
With stirring scents of amaretti strain
Their clam and cannon forms tradition makes,
And crowns with pine-nuts and confetti grain.

The pastry must not be too sweet, nor over-rich the creams;
So must appear the face of life, not lesser than it seems.

Wine-Makers

Eternal life is measured by the wine,
The quality of elixir that flows;
It may engender bitterness in brine
Or crystallize the color of the rose.
The makers pet the soil to plant the seeds
And tenderly their hands caress the vines;
They shape the vineyards and delete the weeds
With deftness splicing stems in clustered lines.
Then, in the season when the fig trees bend,
For need they dance in pairs with grape-stained feet
Or share their crude machine which in the end
Produces wine, the vile, the fair, the sweet.

They show their art, class people to their metered rhyme,
The noble, good, or just the residue in time.

Restaurants

Quo Vadis? To Twelve Caesars' Forum, go,
Beyond the villas, d'Este and Borghese's;
Forsaking Sardi's and Delmonico,
Now sing at Asti's and at Zi Therese's.
At Roma di Notte meet Orsini's crowd
DaVinci painted for Tarello's walls.
Palumbo's Mamma calls Leone loud
To bring the Gino's to Orsatti's halls.
Then drive from Tappan on to Cherry Hill;
See Inns at Fort Side and at Hudson's Bay;
For Fishermen the Wharf is never still
From shore to shore, Four Seasons, night and day.

Their open-fire chefs, Imperatori from the start,
By any name, were Italy's, her cities' cooking art.

Graduation

The father has been busy at the bench;
The mother has kept oiled the pivot, home,
Protecting sons from pills, or glass, or wench;
From piano, books, and stove no daughters roam.
Then comes a starring night in crowning June
When, one by one, with peers the children march.
In academic gowns they step in tune,
Their tensions straining underneath the starch.
Shy father, huddled humbly near the door,
Is stunned to hear his family's name aloud;
The son and daughter win a prize, and, more,
The mother now shakes hands with the endowed.

And so the children's laurels for their parents sign
The list to share with potentates their bread and wine.

The Wedding

How do the years deposit beauty now,
That it perpetuate our ancient strain?
The doe-eyed daughter veils her jet-crowned brow
In white illusions of her wedding train.
A dozen friends in rainbow gowns attend
Her final smiling at her Babbo's arm.
The High Mass and the papal blessing send
Her to the Viking's heir who now is warm.
Sleek-tapered cousins lead her on to dance
In road-house or a whole Astoria floor;
Behind the dolci mounds there is romance
As music-makers let the old tunes soar.

Ciaò, Ciaò, Bambina! Yours is now our carried prize,
The parting future brimming in your father's eyes.

Columbus Day

October is the month of Founder's Day,
The harvest-time to gather up the dream
That set our landsman first upon the way
To agonize the crossing of the stream.
This was the deed that staked the western soil
And charted its possession as our own,
And idlers confiscate to those who toil
To make an edifice where there was stone.
The rustic dynasties we will not watch,
Grandstanding on the streets, and stirring brawls,
Drunk with the froth polluted from their Scotch,
Subverting forums into factioned stalls.

The doer is the maker of the dreams he tries,
And stores for history the facts of enterprise.

Christmas Eve

The earth is hushed; the evening star is still;
The partridges coo low beneath the pass.
The Catskill herdsman leaves his sheep-grazed hill
To reach the village square for midnight Mass.
Each merchant tinsels still his special stall;
All spaces are rent out for season wares;
But our own father's mansion has a hall
To greet us all upon the soft red stairs.
On ours and on the world's own mother's day,
In primo vino god-friends come to dine;
The red fish sauce regales the pasta's way;
The honey on the zeppi mates the wine.

And as the mother rounds to birth her cycled rhyme
She crowns the year in feast, so human is the time.

Epiphany

This is the testament the star shine bears
And leads the Eastern sage to westward plains.
Befana shod, the gift of mystery shares
The truth of childhood where full wisdom reigns.
The giving of a gift is sacred rite,
Committing faith to future love and tie;
It measures invitation the first nite
The neighbors greet the new with them to lie.
It matters not that gifting seeks a shoe
Or gives the heady myrrh, incense, or gold;
It is the magic that the givers do
That makes the children feel a godly hold.

The coming and the giving are lost as useless strife,
Unless the proper witnesses attest their fact in life.

Easter

Their Easter rises like a woman's hand
To fashion a fresh flower on her coat.
The fast is done. Release is in demand
To blow the pipe of every muffled note.
The hallelujahs paganize the Mass
With baritones of morning grappa's sound;
The "Buona Pasqua" grips them to one class,
One outfit, bannered with the wheat they found.
The linen seeps the stain of bread and wine;
The silver cups the strufali, which roll
The honey to the tongue and there confine
The overflow that brims their ancient soul.

The tomb of calumny their destiny defies;
From every death in history they turn and rise.

Gambling

Now, when the angels stopped their game one day,
They found the clouds too soft for rest or sport;
And so reshuffled all the winds to play,
And marked the decks they scattered from their port.
In shapes like boomerangs they reached the West
To light the skies with scraping neon lights;
They made Las Vegas a new kind of rest
For vintners who envision higher sights.
By chance they get to roll the angel's wings,
Who may win hands, stir up a thunder storm;
And when they clap, the whole world spins and sings;
The falling dice give everything its form.

As once they chanced the Rubicon, the cross, the lamp, the hod,
Their numbers rake the stardust falling on their sod.

Our Thing

Say **basta!** to the cultural genocide
The media all wage on them each day;
The nausea vomits greasers' mafioside,
The guineas, dagos, wops, and all who slay.
The nineties in Louisiana bled
Like Sacco and Vanzetti in the North;
Yet Lansky, Schultz, and Moran all have led
To make our thing the scapegoat of their worth.
We will not be the cure-all of the ills
The Brahmin masochist made law;
Our parents taught respect for codes and bills
To letter us as they our future saw.

And now no longer we our Latin lineage shroud,
Admitting to the first of which the rest are proud.

Respectability (Bella Figura)

To have respect from all, a cult has been
With them; so snipes the Time-ly printed page,
Which now, at least, their presence here has seen,
Which erstwhile was indifferent to their rage.
The perfumer distills the scented rose
That penetrates the chemicals of air;
And when the waves in beauty find repose,
The wearer is the flower nursed with care.
And if endemic weeds flaunt parody
With coarse unkeptness, scruffing breeding's hand,
They mock, thus, what was once necessity
When gardeners lacked the tools to mulch the sand.

The timeless pride of self directs its saving pace,
As clothing is the image of the inner face.

Opera

Brave Gatti Casazza built the opera house
Where drama, costume, music voiced and met;
He tapped a glory with a baton's douse
And for the golden West the boxes set.
All heard Mascagni, Verdi, Bellini,
Leoncovallo's clown, Enrico's heart,
Giovanni as Alfredo, sweet Puccini,
With all the Toscas singing every part.
We waifed with them along Parisian streets
And marched to die upon the sacred Nile;
And now Menotti's saint the medium beats
With Persichetti's Genesis in style.

The genius which rebirthed all arts for one to hold
Created so the form in which it could be told.

Singing

Like troubadours in groves beneath the stars,
They brush stray tears that stain the picnic board;
And, strumming mandolins and old guitars,
They pick their memories to strike each chord.
Sul Ponte di Bassano they once found
Un Mazzolin di Fiori on way Mari;
The Alpine flower Sul Cappello round
They sing for San' Lucia far at sea.
Vieni sul mar, my bella romanina,
Al di là, we'll find O sole mio.
And Non Dimenticare, Ciaò, bambina,
Some mattinata, soon, return to me.

Addio, anima e core, Napoli we sing
Arrivederci Rome, we cry **volare** on the wing.

Popular Singers

They taught the nation's singing how to rise
Above the ditty, wail, and nursery rhyme.
Their songs are sirens culling them with ties
To their strange shores with harmonies in time.
The opera stars recalled the old bay tunes;
Then, others sang along with radio.
Sinatra, Bennett, Como, each one croons;
Damone, Martino, Vale, and Martin go
On records, where no melody is wrong;
And sounds beat rhythms measured in true time,
Returning to Sorrento in their song
To find again the love that lives in rhyme.

They sing the words while others turn the tunes to dance;
They give the sound the concert lore of old romance.

HALL OF FAME

Enrico Tonti (1650-1704)

Enrico Tonti had an iron hand
To budge the paths to guide his friend LaSalle.
The great Sieur dreamed a New World's Empire land
With pelts to gild the royal court and hall.
The first of Europe's sons in Arkansas,
He went to Montreal to aid the braves;
Defeating Iroquois in rebel war,
He went to save the French from massive graves.
For lost LaSalle he strengthened Frontenac;
The fevered Mississippi was his gauge,
That rolled his memoires, read by king and hack,
And for Louisiana built the stage.

Gaeta's son, he built for France a regal trade and name;
But, with America's first homes, as man he laid a claim.

Philippo Mazzei (1730-1816)

Philippo Mazzei, freedom's voice and phrase,
Enflamed with tongue of fire on the hill
The thoughts of Jefferson for many days,
And wrote the words as nearly they are still.
He planted first the vineyards for our wine,
The golden citrus, peaceful olive trees;
And then his spirit sparked his thundering line
For lightning war to storm democracies.
Men are, said he, by nature equally free
And independent, equal in their rights.
All men are created equal we agree,
And used his plan that won at Yorktown Heights.

He paved the way with letters, words, and vine
For Thomas Paine, the conversazioni, and the wine.

Constantino Brumidi (1805-1880)

Brumidi, were you here with us today,
Apotheosis of our Washington!
The fresco frieze with landmarks still is gray;
Armed Liberty with shield and sword is done.
Our Graeco-Roman Michelangelo
Led Cincinnatus from the plow to Rome;
Fixed next to Putnam who to war would go
For independence, stairways leading home.
Vespucci, Brewster, Franklin, Columbus,
Cornwallis pounced with old mythology;
You brought the palace classics here to us
To altars bared by ideology.

You dreamed to meld old Romans and the new country,
The only place where beauty ages liberty.

Luigi Palma di Cesnola (1832-1904)

Luigi Palma di Cesnola, Count,
Was Lincoln's battle star at Oldie Gap;
No rebel thief his boots could search, nor mount
The general's steed to rape the Union map.
Aristocrat of stately height and power,
Charmed others into love of duty's pain;
As consul in old Cypress brought to flower
The buried artifacts the Turks would gain.
The treasured vaults of Temples he brought home,
Creating art of housing art in city walls;
The Metropolitan could then become,
Like its director, first among the halls.

He claimed the pride of race he said that none surpassed,
Discoverers whose names by works are made to last.

St. Frances Xavier Cabrini (1850-1917)

The doves fly high above the eagle's nest
From Lombardy to far Columbia's shore;
They soar "not to the East, but to the West,"
To graft the apple seed to God once more.
The new world's crown is by Cabrini worn,
Who sheds her sixty-seven veils to show
The humble, the infirm, the children torn,
That spirit from the frail makes giants grow.
As Frances with the lords and birds commands,
She honors arrogance with no complaint;
The waters of West Park flow to her hands:
This woman immigrant is our first saint.

The holy Mathers, wary Franklins to her ethic get
Direction; for, in Asia, suns of old no longer set.

A. P. Giannini (1870-1949)

A. P. Giannini, son of San Jose,
Stood up six feet to commandeer the gold,
To leave its realm and round the worker's way
Where little men need little rings to hold.
His money had a human force and scale;
The birthday fives were saved and put to work;
Bancitaly, in wagon loads, the hail
Of earthquake stood, and stirred the Morgan's irk.
The Transamerica, near undermined
By Walker, Calkins, blues against the white,
The proxy battle won in Wall Street's bind,
Then launched the Golden Gate to bridge the fight.

The largest branch the serviced people hold,
America, that banks the world in gold.

Enrico Caruso (1873-1921)

Caruso, song immortal and still clear,
Whose sound could ravish fingers of the blind
And mute. The timbres of the rooftops bear
The flawless pitch that scales the reach of mind.
Sweet boy contralto, Naples' blessed son,
A mother's gift to opera's altar stone;
He sang to fame the Metropolitan
And dignified the playful gramaphone.
First victor of the record industry,
Where other artists followed with his move,
Inspiring others was his ministry;
His voice survived the elixir of love.

A star he was to flame above the rest;
And when he gave his song, it was the best.

Rudolph Valentino (1895-1926)

First star to light the darkened film of night,
He raised the Latin from the railbed's ditch
To climb the polar stair and lift his sight
To where he might his pick and stoneboat hitch.
The Neapolitan for us the image changed
From green-horned chickweeds to exotic fruit.
The lover in Arabian nights arranged
That he the dream of every dreamer suit.
The women danced with him in fancy's room
The Tango, rhythm's passion with an arm;
The men, admiring shieks, with Nordic gloom,
Detained and feted him at Wolfe's Neck's farm.

Suave Valentino, herald of the new world's art and love,
Forever set the reel to which our own romances move.

Fiorello H. La Guardia (1882-1947)

The biggest little man the country reared
From Arizona's sands came back to guard
The Halls of old New York; the Tiger feared
The fighting pint that boiled the melting ward.
Insurgent, breaking power, gold, and fame,
The first Acadian set to freak a seat,
In Congress, burning favor like a flame,
A flying warrior with major beat,
With his Gibboni, rounding Camelot
The regular they squared with right;
Fought Mellon, Muscle Shoals, and bogging rot
To unpollute the land of racial blight.

The little flower more a giant lies
Than bloated bud that with his promise dies.

Enrico Fermi (1901-1954)

Man's genius greater is than he can know,
As is the scent unwatered to the rose.
The artist never to his art can grow;
Columbus sails to lands that no map shows.
Enrico Fermi, navigator, too,
Unlocked the door to the Atomic Age,
Though Nobel Prized, did more than, doing, knew
When he in Rome in thirty-four was sage.
Columbia's pile, Chicago's Met Lab massed
For him to start the chain-reaction bomb,
The "Trinity" the whole world saw, aghast,
One hundred Fermium for peace or doom.

Italian navigation is a mercury
That sets new worlds to work the future's destiny.

John O. Pastore (1907-   )

The shepherd guards the stations by the hours
And stays awake that free men still may know
That apes chant filth and leap upon the towers
To slice the lines and twist transmitters low.
He hears the sounds of battle in the air,
The screech that jams so reason only hums,
The bursts of blasting of the ears made bare
And strangled by the noise and noose of drums.
The gentle Pastore veers the brutal spears
That would dissect communication's heart
To use the waves as weapons of their jeers
And plunder what they had no mind to start.

The Senator with ancient echoes still is heard,
The thumb poised sure upon the trigger of the word.

Dan Mitrione, American Civilian Police Advisor in Uruguay
(Martyred by Tupamaros, July 31, 1970)

Dan Mitrione, contemporary man,
Defender of the young who courtrooms fill,
Policed as chief the grateful Richmond clan
And cared to Horizonte in Brazil;
Was our advisor to the Uruguay
With AID to fight guerrilla urban reds.
The Tupamaros murdered him their way,
Blackmailing terror over peoples' heads.
The Radlibs here give trial to patriots,
Our heroes, dying martyrs where they roam;
The Senate's Church checks out to soothe the sots,
The mocking chic, the tribunates at home.

The tube is loosely balled with Al Capones
But finds untouchable the Mitriones.

Joseph Alioto, the Mayor (1916-)

This Alioto for us all stands tall,
A Eucalyptus grown from ancient seed,
To cast a shade that some a shadow call
Upon the lines that film the broken breed.
To splice the worm-taped look, he blots its life;
And slide falls after slide upon the heap.
His giant leaves so choke the weeds in strife,
He needs no creature's dung his stem to keep.
He sweats away the poisons of his roots
That swelled infection from a bitter soil;
Where he would prune the boughs of suckling shoots
The law instructs and girds him in its coil.

This quickened tree, ripe in its forest bower,
Must crown the wood, the shading and the power.

Mario Puzo (1920-)

Alone and crestless, in your house you sat,
While love and children lived below your room;
You conjured all the malice, envy's brat,
With which the scribblers balled your mother's bloom.
So raged you were by their relentless twist
To denigrate Acadia's noble line,
You dug into their script and slashed their wrist
To magnify what bled their own decline.
From all the storms of all our discontents,
You rolled our snow into one giant ball;
You coated it with ice of their pretense,
And hit their face to smash them from our mall.

From under boots of petrified Borboni
You resurrect the rights of all Corleoni.

CONCLUSIONS

Nonna

La Nonna plies away on her crochet
As others litigate in voices shrill;
She smiles, for she still has her say
When Poppa's anger ebbs before her will.
She says, "Sta' zit ! Here comes ma friend next door,
Zi' Solomon'—he brings the besta thread
To make the spread my Cumma' Bridget' saw,
For Milton and Leonora's marriage bed.
And Gumpa' Fritz he comma to see you here
And talk about old time on Union Hill;
He likes your wine, so better than his beer.
He izza 'u nòn to Rosie's littla Bill.

Zi' Solomon', whatta y' mean, the birds they fly witha one feather?
Gesù, Giuseppe, Maria! We carry da crossa in America together!"

By-Line, June 29, 1971

And yet Vanzetti bleeds with Sacco still
As brutes without a conscience hang the courts,
And both the ring and square the dancers fill;
The obscene lie the charted law aborts.
Behold the monkey-mouth which apes the moors,
While silenced heroes spear their own right side.
All hear the final slamming of the doors
Of children who with Christ have law-crossed died.
The jaded cast, black gowns now sewn in pink,
Would dance a jig in operetta time
To center-stage the thief, and let all think
That treason is supreme, the act sublime.

And while the quaking cowards hide beneath the rust,
Who names the law Colombo broke to bite the dust?

Politics

Cry Mafia! and plague the candidate,
That he by any darkened foe be felled.
Insinuate he knows the syndicate
That from the polls his name may so be held,
Although the waspish pirates manned the seas
And murdered reds, and chained the bartered blacks,
And robbing barons piled monopolies
With martial hands, then registered their hacks,
The small reformer clerking on his stools
Sent forth his sister to enroll in pleas
Against the Latin names in streets and schools;
He feared they might expose his hobbling knees.

With Morte Alla Francia, Italians Allied, freedom won;
Within the Bay, no IRA, Alioto goes—right on!

The Builders

Now, look where once our fathers laid the tracks
And picked and shoveled bowels of the earth.
They steer the rivers, build the factory stacks
With stones and steel; they bind the city's girth.
Their Bronxville homes are of their own design;
They own the castles guarding Riverside;
And in the Hall of Dons they drink the wine
To toast the vessels on the Bay's right side.
Though concrete crucified their missioned limbs
And monuments from quarries guard their bones,
The buildings are cathedrals of their hymns
Composed in choired notes of bricks and stones.

These are the hands that stamp the nation's strength and size;
They mold her worldwide power with their enterprise.

The Men in Business

They now preside and chair large companies,
The Pittstown, Flintkote, Tropicana, Crane,
Ford, Chrysler, Fedders, U.S. Industries,
The Sperry Hutchinson, the Borden chain.
From South Pacific, Rochester with phones,
America, the Bank and the Skyline,
Commute the Admirals and the Houdáille drones,
The Stock Exchange, the makers of the wine.
With cars and stamps and rails for mobile home
They organize the land's new expertise,
And where they worked cow dung to ply the loam
They now are major cotters of the cheese.

Where once they laid the tracks to oil the baronies,
They've crossed to syndicate their own monopolies.

Italian-American Novelists
(with poetic license)

Arleo, Basso, Benasutti, Buranelli,
Calitri, Canizio, Canzoneri, Corsel, Ciambelli,
Caruso, Caudela, Cenedella, Creatore, M. DeCapite,
Cuomo, D'Agostino, D'Angelo, DeVoto, R. DeCapite,
DeLillo, DiDonato, Fante, Fumente, Forgione,
Gallico, Ianuzzi, Lapolla, Longo, Mangione,
Mirabelli, Miceli, Moroso, Panetta,
Pagano, Papaleo, Pollini, Pasinetti,
Pronzini, Pillitteri, Piazza, Puzo, Radano
Sorrentino, Savo, Savarese, Stefano,
Talese, Tomasi, Trocchi, Tucci, Valenti,
Ventura, Vergara, Villa, Winwar, Vivante.

You mean, there is an Italian-American novelist?
There are books that now authenticate this list.

Social Status

They care not much. For what is there to gain?
There are some sons of Sons of Italy
Who flaunt The Winged Foot upon the train,
Pay dues to country clubs too hastily.
But most are like old Boston's Cabotti,
Who still prefer compounded family,
Augmenting lineage with the Braggiotti,
See Colonna to Carloni steadily.
The Tagliaferro southern aristocracy
Are blacksmiths to the crackers Tollifer;
The quiet dons of our democracy
A social world invisible prefer.

If status be the fruit of public charity,
They live that way by nature, without registry.

And Now

The Romans are serene in Scarsdale now
Where vine leaves crush petunias and old phlox;
And quatrains that once smoothed the poet's plow
Are now reversed to vision in a box.
The ancient bread has multiplied its forms,
And mellowed wine has melted ice and foam
To quicken still the sounds of vocal norms
With which the art of music is at home.
The daughters grace as wives the Saxon clans;
The sons replace the corporate heads in town,
As gently still the continental hands
Drive on the roads they built with steel they own.

And deep behind the wounded shadows of their eyes
The drill-call spear of human knowledge ready lies.

Projection

You shall resist the unrelenting pride
And hold all condescension in contempt;
Allow them at their crest a while to ride
Who from the thatch and bog are here exempt.
The memory lies fixed within your eyes
Of having kept supremacy in rein;
The turning wheels and hands have no surprise
For you who engineered the tracks and train.
Three times you led the powers of the sphere,
By law, by spirit, and humanity;
You will reject by truth the slander here,
Untouchable in your integrity.

For though the aphids may consume one year the rose,
Another year the sturdy stem another blossom blows.

Ethnicized

I wander on the dark side of the moon,
Because my father left the noonday sun;
The New World shuns the middle afternoon,
Seducing star-shine for its morning run.
The images of hills in Apennines
Are fading into shadows in the glass;
What once were holy hymns in Roman pines
Are siren songs of smoke from potted grass.
The rumblings of the city now suffice
To group-fix all the lynching gangs of sham;
They bleed us to another age of ice
To prove that "I was more than what I am."

In history the hyphen cancels out my ethnic face;
No footnote marks the meteor so doubly lost in space.

Ethnic Slurs

The rift that English has from Latin root
Is one mere sibilant, a consonant,
Like an abrasive that an extinct brute
Retained to ante an impediment.
Just as, near ancient seas, a maid turned swine,
Seducing ears with winged hissing sound,
There was, in turn, reduced to Roman wine
The word the bee-lined cork no longer bound.
Then, later still, when insects sailed the seas
Along with bonded sons of soil and shop,
Too, With Out Passage came the Southern ease
To brief the Wasp and bed him with a Wop.

Reality removes excessive claims,
Deletes the letters of divisive names.

Declaration

Our compatriot, a Mediterranean,
Through Albion sought the Potomac shore;
And word by word instructed Jefferson
The old Republic's borrowed book and core.
Our happiness in life is liberty;
Semantics triple what we know is one;
The Roman word defies hypocrisy
And equals in fraternity are won.
The Constitution flaunts no mono-words,
To flush the barnyards, cat-pads, and latrines;
It shines the stars of mind to post the roads
To verbal sky-tops where the immortal leans.

The freedoms stored in classics our common clauses bear
And words we say our levels both in sight and sound declare.

Americadians, Out-of-Place

Italians in America renew
The issues of ancestral pedagogues;
Their children, now, in libraries review
The lethal words of ancient dialogues.
They have explored endemic reasons why
They rate as orphans of establishment
And found that in the mother-land still cry
The fledglings born of ravaged sentiment.
As strangers here, they hewed a nation's saint
To foster them from island fence and brute;
Their children now give more without restraint
Than could the native gentry follow suit.

Since neither nation gives them filial pride
They are the foundlings of the father's bride.

Return to Rome

I have come home again to walk once more
Beyond the gates along the Appian Way.
I touch the ground where fathers marched before,
And cross the Tiber where my spirits stay.
Inside the Forum, voices on the wind
Recall the logic of my smoothed-out speech.
The unchained Muses luminate my mind
And wing their poetry within my reach.
Where Hadrian arched the road from every foam
And carried bread for circus men at play,
The wine of God was in the mind of Rome;
Aurelius first by reason marked the way.

The stones are polished by the circling sphere;
The end and the beginning both are here.

The Italo-American

Who is an Italo-American
What is ethnicity that hyphenates?
A young adult is going home again
To forge the keys to ply the welded gates.
The hammer he had used to smash the locks
Fell haplessly into the boiling pot;
It could not bend a shape to split the rocks
That walled the fortress over drying rot.
But, when he thrust his claw to work alone
Beyond the moat, whose bank led to the South,
He found the waters fouled, the bridges gone,
An exile docked upon the river's mouth.

He winds his way, back to the watershed,
The source from which the other streams have fed.

Becoming an American

Although I cried at birth in New Rochelle
And nursed my growth on cold New England hills,
I felt the Brahmin's story did not tell
The truth—America in rocks and rills.
My father bore New Jersey's spit and shame
Until he broke the barrier of the sound;
He then surpassed his father in the game
To be a patriot to the ivy-gowned.
They filmed my brain that I might see
That here the oracle its truth would bring;
But I, in clearer sight by each degree,
Have seen the negative blur everything.

The truth is that I really am at home
When once I learn I am the child of Rome.

Bibliography (Selected for Reference)

Las Vegas publishes first Caesars now;
Facsimiles of Nero Camden has.
Augustus', seers and saints, in rare books show
Young Augie how the world of glory was.
Allighieri's vision shelved at Dante's Place,
Mark Anthony, a saint in Tony's Room,
Are strange Borgheses, glitter in a case,
To cream the volumes, Medicis to bloom.
With Cicero, the Bourbons, classified,
Group by Chicago in a misspelled word;
Pasquale's name, to honor though they tried,
Became the nation's Patsy, read and heard.

The son of Rome's old Senate has here become a busman.
But who deserves the footnote when Musmanno is a Musmann?

Coda

There is an index to their living code,
Inscrutable as Mona Lisa's smile.
The shadow of their brow can still forbode:
Their knowing eyes will scan the world a while.
Two thousand years of reparations borne
For having sacked the serpent's poison mesh,
Extracting from the scalp a brain so torn,
They sank its tooth to pierce the human flesh.
And when they bled the venom with their sword
And healed the gashes with their sainted scars,
They left their law briefs and their guarded word
To hit the fox, the maker of the wars.

And so with art and families the best of self they drive
That others may drink beauty and the human pit survive.